A Day in the Life Of

# A Tree

Ruby Tuesday Books

Ruth Owen

Little Acorns

**Published in 2025 by Ruby Tuesday Books Ltd.**



Editor: Mark J. Sachner
Design: Tammy West
Production: John Lingham

**Photo Credits:**
Alamy: 16 (Bill Gozansky); Shutterstock: Cover (Zerbor), 4 (George Trumpeter & Zerbor), 5 (Mike Ver Sprill, 1mboromom, Steve Byland, markusmayer, Jeff Rzepka, & Feng Yu), 6 (Mykhailo Pavlenko), 7, 8 (Lina7471), 9T (Dudarev Mikhail), 9B (Rodion Golova), 10 (Zerbor), 11 (Buslik), 12 (Yuri Antonenko), 13 (leonardo2011), 14 (New Africa), 15 (Valentina Razumova), 17 (Harry Collins Photography), 18 (Valeriya Rychkova), 19 (Marilyn Barbone), 20 (Ohishiapply & Zerbor), 21 (Rudmer Zwerver), 22 (ABC photographs, Semmick Photo, & Willee Cole Photography), 23 (showcake, kaczor58, & Gabriele Rohde), 24 (Alexandr Shevchenko).

Library of Congress Control Number: 2024941199

Print (Hardback) ISBN 978-1-78856-504-2
Print (Paperback) ISBN 978-1-78856-505-9
ePub ISBN 978-1-78856-506-6

Published in Minneapolis, MN
Printed in the United States

**www.rubytuesdaybooks.com**

# CONTENTS

# Welcome to a New Day!

It's morning, and the Sun is rising.

A loud, happy noise comes from the leafy **branches** of an oak tree.

The birds that live in the oak tree are singing.

Their songs say

welcome to a new day!

Clouds float over the oak tree.

Rain falls from the clouds
and soaks into the ground.

The tree's **roots** suck up rainwater from under the ground.

The oak tree drinks a bathtub of water each day.

The water flows from the tree's roots up its **trunk.**

The tree's trunk is covered with **bark**.

The water flows along the tree's thick branches.

It flows into thin twigs and into the leaves.

Now the tree's leaves have a special job to do.

They make sweet, sugary food for the tree!

The leaves make food with water, **gas** from the air,

The sweet food gives the tree energy.

It uses the energy to grow new branches, twigs, and leaves.

The tree also grows acorns.

The acorns will turn brown and fall to the ground.

Last fall, the tree's acorns fell to the ground.

Now the oak tree has a little neighbor.

It's a baby oak tree!

It is growing from one of the acorns.

An acorn is an oak tree **seed**.

The oak tree is like an animal town.

Squirrels live in a hole in the tree's trunk.

This hole is home to a woodpecker family!

All day, the tree makes food in its leaves.

It also helps make the air that we breathe.

The tree's leafy branches make cool shade.

When the Sun goes down, tiny nighttime animals fly from the tree.

# Bats!

Bats live in little cracks in the tree's bark.

The oak tree's busy day is over.

# Glossary

**bark**
A tough, rough covering that protects a tree's trunk and branches.

**branch**
A long part of a tree that grows from the trunk. Twigs, leaves, flowers, and fruits grow from branches.

**gas**
A substance in the air that we can't see. People and animals breathe gases in and out.

**roots**

Underground parts of a plant. Roots take in water and hold a plant in the soil.

**seed**

A tiny part of a plant that contains everything needed to grow a new plant.

**trunk**

The thick main stem of a tree.

# Index